AWESOME INVENTIONS
You Use EVERY DAY

TREMENDOUS TECHNOLOGY INVENTIONS

KATIE MARSICO

LERNER PUBLICATIONS COMPANY
MINNEAPOLIS

Lerner Publications Company
A division of Lerner Publishing Group, Inc.
241 First Avenue North
Minneapolis, MN 55401 U.S.A.

Website address: www.lernerbooks.com

Library of Congress Cataloging-in-Publication Data

Marsico, Katie, 1980–
Tremendous technology inventions /
by Katie Marsico.
p.   cm. — (Awesome inventions you use
every day)
Includes index.
ISBN 978–1–4677–1092–3 (lib. bdg. : alk. paper)
ISBN 978–1–4677–1690–1 (eBook)
1. Inventions—Juvenile literature. 2. Technological
innovations—Juvenile literature. I. Title.
T48.M386 2014
600—dc23   2012046008

Manufactured in the United States of America
1 – PP – 7/15/13

CONTENTS

INTRODUCTION:

GOTTA <3 TECHNOLOGY!

Screens—you gotta love 'em! Face it. You touch them. You watch them. They make it easy and fun to find your way around the digital world we live in. Inventors have come up with a lot of cool screen technology. Yet it is more than just cool. Have you ever thought about life without these inventions?

Oh, the horror of not texting your friends! And how would you feel about copying two hundred flyers for the school bake sale by hand? Sore and cranky to say the least!

That's only the tip of the iceberg. Swoosh your fingers across your smartphone and you can order pizza and listen to your favorite pop star. Yes, with screen technology, you can pretty much rule the world. So get set to learn about ten amazing inventions and why you are lucky to have them. You can start reading as soon as that song ends.

COPY MACHINES

Time for a history quiz! Which of these statements is true? a) Thomas Jefferson wrote the Declaration of Independence. b) He was the third president of the United States. c) He used a copier. d) All of the above. Pencils down! Did you choose "all of the above"? That's the right answer!

Jefferson did not own a Xerox machine. He worked with a copying press. In 1780 inventor James Watt developed this early mechanical copier. (Watt also designed the steam engine.)

To use the press, a person would place a damp sheet of paper against a document. A heavy block pressed both sheets of paper together. The ink from the document transferred to the damp paper. The words showed up backward. So you had to read the copy by flipping over the paper and looking through its back side.

Sound like a lot of work? It was! A lawyer in New York named Chester Carlson wanted an easier way to make copies. In the late 1930s, he began working on a process called xerography. Carlson's method did not require liquids. Instead, his machine used static electricity, light, and a powder called toner to make dry copies. The copier electrically charged words on a piece of paper. Then it shined light on the words. Toner formed the print on the paper. In 1959 the company that later became Xerox started selling Carlson's machine.

Zip ahead more than fifty years. Your mom's clinic, your dad's office, and your school all have copiers and laser printers. These machines are complex. Yet they make our lives a lot simpler. Want proof? One study showed that people pump out 3.1 *trillion* copies and laser-printed pages every year!

Does this copier look like a modern copy machine? Nope. It's a portable copier that President Thomas Jefferson made in the early 1800s.

Heat and electrical charges—that's what this Xerox copier (RIGHT) from the 1960s needed to do its job.

TELEVISIONS

It's Saturday morning. You want to watch your favorite cartoon shows. You search your house from top to bottom. There's no television in sight. This has to be a bad dream! How will you live without TV?

Calm down. That was just to show you what life would be like if no one had invented TV. But fortunately for you, someone did!

Early inventors were not worried about making cartoon fans happy. Men like Alexander Graham Bell wanted to find a way to link sounds with sights. Bell is best known for inventing the telephone in 1876. He also hoped to find a way to let callers see the person on the other end of the line.

Bell was not the only person interested in connecting sound and vision. Popular trading cards from the 1890s show a machine that would allow audiences of the future to watch and listen to live concerts from home.

So who took the next step to create television? One of these people was Philo Taylor Farnsworth. He was in high school in Idaho when he first thought about such an invention.

Farnsworth knew the first step was to capture a moving image with a camera. Next, he needed to code this image into radio waves. Then he had to change the image back into a picture that could be shown on a screen.

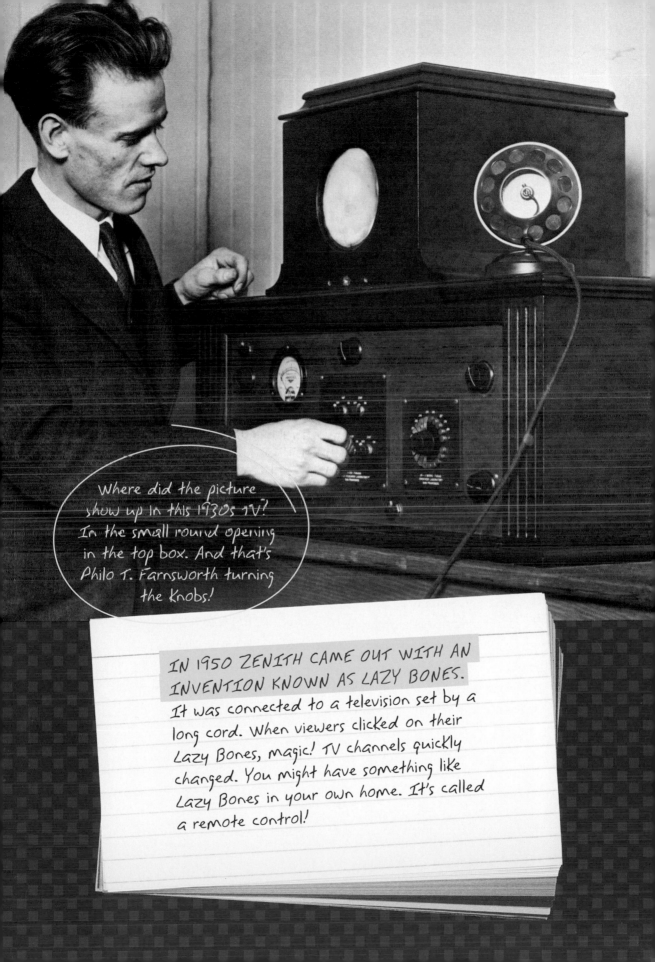

Where did the picture show up in this 1930s TV? In the small round opening in the top box. And that's Philo T. Farnsworth turning the knobs!

IN 1950 ZENITH CAME OUT WITH AN INVENTION KNOWN AS LAZY BONES. It was connected to a television set by a long cord. When viewers clicked on their Lazy Bones, magic! TV channels quickly changed. You might have something like Lazy Bones in your own home. It's called a remote control!

Farnsworth found a way to carry out these steps. He used a beam of electrons to scan images onto a screen. In 1927 he created a special camera tube. He worked with it to broadcast a simple image of lines onto a screen in his lab. Farnsworth went on to capture an image of a dollar sign and another of his wife's face.

Later, the Radio Corporation of America (RCA) spent $50 million to build on Farnsworth's work for television. By 1939 people were watching TV broadcasts of the New York World's Fair and college baseball games. In 1955 half of all U.S. homes had a TV. Viewers tuned in to watch the news and their favorite actors and comedians.

Meanwhile, inventors kept busy. For example, they introduced color TV to Americans in the early 1950s. Cable television became popular by the mid-1970s. Inventors also figured out new ways to give audiences a better picture and sound. Modern TV screens are made from liquid crystals and millions of tiny gas cells called plasma. This makes for super-clear pictures.

Of course, you probably don't just watch TV on the set in your living room. Viewers stream their favorite shows and live video onto another tremendous tech invention—the computer!

Watching TV in the 1950s was a family affair. And TV shows were in black and white.

Modern TVs have lots of cool features. Huge screens, great color, and remote controls are just a few!

COMPUTERS

How big is the computer you usually use? Can you stuff it into your backpack or hold it in your hand? You couldn't carry around the Mark I computer. This early computer stretched 51 feet (16 meters) long and 8 feet (2.4 m) tall! Howard Aiken built the Mark I in 1944. The U.S. military used it to calculate how to fire weapons.

Humans have used machines to do calculations for thousands of years. For example, ancient peoples did math with an abacus. It was made from rods and beads.

By the 1800s, people were using paper punch cards. Holes punched into the cards in certain patterns were a way to store and track data. In the 1880s, Herman Hollerith made a machine that could read punch cards. He used the machine to track the population of the United States. In 1924 Hollerith's company changed its name to International Business Machines (IBM).

In the 1930s, German inventor Konrad Zuse wanted to make a calculating machine. So he designed the Z1 in his parents' living room. He created this computer with many of the same parts you have in your own computer. The Z1 had mechanical memory to store data. It was programmed to figure out math problems using a code made up of 0s and 1s.

The Z1 relied on a motor and a hand crank to work. Inventors later built computers that ran on electric power. They also designed electrical circuits called chips. Computer chips store a lot of information in a tiny space.

Can you believe how gigantic the Mark I computer was? It had hundreds of miles of wire and weighed 10,000 pounds (4,535 kilograms)!

Computers of the 1940s and 1950s were huge. Most were made for math and science labs. They were not built for kids who wanted to play computer games or type book reports.

This changed in the 1960s. Douglas Engelbart invented the computer mouse, hypertext, and graphical user interface (GUI—pronounced "gooey"). It's thanks to him that you can give your computer a command by clicking on a picture on your screen. Engelbart's ideas came to life with personal computers (PCs). These desktop computers hit store shelves in the 1970s and the 1980s.

PCs were much smaller than the Mark I. They were meant for just one user at a time. Smaller laptops and handheld computers followed in the 1990s and the early 2000s. They are proof that bigger is not always better. Most people prefer computers they can carry with them.

Yet there are still some amazing monsters out there. Check out IBM's supercomputer Sequoia. It covers 3,000 square feet (280 sq. m). That's as big as a large two-story house! Sequoia is the world's fastest computer. Scientists use it to solve more than sixteen *quadrillion* calculations per second!

WHO SAYS INVENTORS HAVE TO BE BEST BUDS?

Bill Gates is the founder of the software company Microsoft. Steve Jobs ruled a different computer world—Apple. Both men shaped how people use computers. Both made billions of dollars. They even hung out together in the 1980s.

But Gates and Jobs were two of the world's toughest rivals. And they did not always say nice things about each other. Gates did not think Jobs knew much about technology. Jobs said he thought Microsoft made junky products. But both men respected each other's brilliant thinking. And Gates even told Jobs so in a letter Jobs had by his bed when he died in 2011.

Bill Gates in 1986

Steve Jobs in 1984

VIDEO GAMES

Are you a big fan of Mario? How about Zelda? Or tic-tac-toe? You might be surprised to learn that video games began with a bunch of Xs and Os.

British inventor A. S. Douglas developed an electronic version of tic-tac-toe in 1952. Yet Douglas was more interested in research than after-school fun. He wanted to use his game to study the way humans and computers communicate.

Luckily, other inventors were thinking outside the lab. These scientists started coming up with video and computer programs that could be used for entertainment. Inventors created arcade games and home-gaming consoles in the 1960s and the 1970s. Players used paddles and joysticks to control the computer systems behind video-game magic.

Zoom ahead to the twenty-first century. Motion sensors and cameras are part of many hi-tech game systems. So are touch screens and 3-D graphics. Want to see how good a gamer you really are? You can test your skills against players all around the world with online gaming!

You may not have to go that far for tough competition though. Your little sister is probably better at *Angry Birds* than you think. Some of the 64 million kids who play video games are only two years old!

With these games, they can experience life in war zones and army camps. They use virtual technology to learn what different landscapes look like and to learn how to fire weapons. Players can even practice flying military planes and driving tanks.

Paddle or Wii remote? In the 1970s, it took a paddle to fight off aliens in the *Space Invaders* video game (TOP). To play Wii baseball (RIGHT), just pick up your Wii remote and swing!

THE INTERNET

You are not one in a million. It is more like one in 2.3 *billion*. That's the total number of people who use the Internet. Maybe you send a couple of the 250 billion e-mails that go out every day. You probably also use the Internet to find fast facts for school projects and reports. Or maybe you go online to learn how the home team is doing in today's doubleheader.

The Internet dates back to the 1960s. Many tech wizards helped build this global computer network. At first, inventors wanted to link government, business, and university computers. They knew that this would be a faster way to share information.

Over time, scientists got busy linking home computers to the Internet too. British scientist Tim Berners-Lee developed the World Wide Web in 1991. This invention lets people all around the world read and view all kinds of information online.

Berners-Lee and great thinkers like him made it easy for you to surf the Web and fire off e-mails. They built a user-friendly online world that brings a whole lot of folks together. Sound a bit warm and fuzzy? Here's a hard, cold fact instead. In the time it took you to read the last few sentences, about twenty million electronic messages zoomed across the Internet!

If you want, you can send an electronic message to everyone from the pope to Bill Gates. You can even go online to fire off fan mail to Homer Simpson!

The Internet connects people on all continents all around the world.

Tim Berners-Lee (RIGHT) invented the World Wide Web. He dreams of a day when machines will talk to machines to do our daily tasks. Could this include homework?!

GLOBAL POSITIONING SYSTEMS

What's worse than running late for a big soccer game? Your mom getting lost on the way there! Take a deep breath. After all, you have a Global Positioning System (GPS) on your side. Your mom hits a button on her cell phone before you leave home. The phone spits out a map showing exactly how to get to the game. It even provides spoken directions for her to follow! Soon you're zooming toward the field.

You might think the best part of this story is that you make it to your game on time. Yet it's also pretty cool that you and your mom can use satellite power to find your way there. GPS figures out where you are by tracking how long it takes for different satellite signals from space to reach your car.

Airplanes and boats also use GPS. So do a lot of laptop computers and construction equipment. The U.S. military came up with GPS in the 1970s. The military uses GPS to find targets and guide weapons. It also relies on GPS to locate pilots whose planes have been shot down.

Most people use GPS to get directions. GPS can also tell you how far you have traveled. It can even predict when you will get where you are going.

GPS units are pretty good at their jobs too. They are superaccurate—and superfast. For example, it takes only sixty-five to eighty-five milliseconds for signals to pass between a satellite and a GPS unit back on Earth. Then again, every millisecond counts when a soccer game is at stake!

MP3 PLAYERS

What are your top ten favorite songs? Quick! Scroll across the screen of an iPod. Some models hold up to forty thousand songs. Most models are also small enough to fit inside your pocket. Your iPod will even tell you what songs you listen to most. Bingo!

The iPod is one example of an MP3 player. These digital audio players store and play music. Many of them also store photos and play videos.

British inventor Kane Kramer was designing digital players as far back as the 1970s. This was long before you could surf the Web. Kramer dreamed of using phone lines and portable electronics to order music and videos on demand.

Yet the world was not ready for Kramer's device. In 1979 a memory chip could store only about 3.5 minutes of music. And you couldn't buy and download music online.

About twenty years later, a company in South Korea started selling the first digital music player. MPMan could hold only about six songs and was not a huge hit. That's changed because of iPods and other players that have come out since MPMan. Many of these players are built right into smartphones, such as the iPhone. By 2012 fans of Apple's iPods and iPhones were downloading 1.3 million songs from its online music store every twenty-four hours!

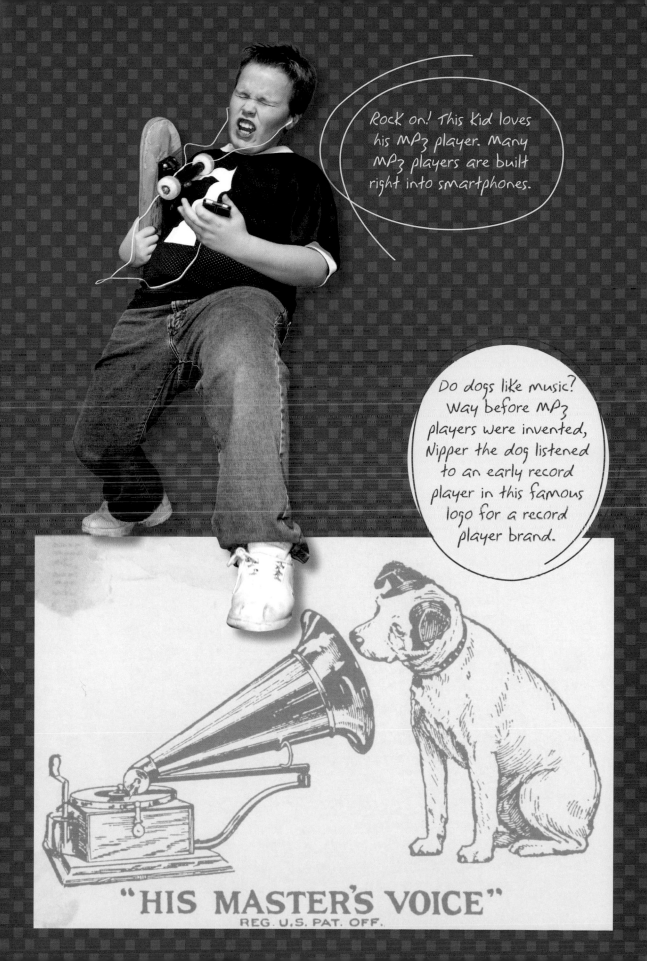

E-READERS

The bell rings. You wait for your teacher to drop a mountain of books on your desk. Instead, she hands you a thin electronic device about the size of a spiral notebook. Has the world run out of paper? Has your teacher gone crazy?

This story actually happened in Canada in 2009. It was the first time a school replaced paper textbooks with e-readers. The truth is that e-readers are not just classroom tools. You might have used one to catch up on *Diary of a Wimpy Kid*.

E-readers have been around since the early 1970s. But they weren't portable. So the folks at Sony got to work and created the Data Discman in 1992. This was the first portable device for reading e-books. Yet not everyone went wild for the Data Discman. A lot of people said that the screen was difficult to read—especially in sunlight. And it was big.

Since then, e-readers have become much easier to use. They are small and lightweight. In fact, by 2011, more buyers were choosing e-books than print books. Do you think print books will be the next dinosaurs?

Johannes Gutenberg made the first printed book—a Bible (LEFT)—in 1455.

WANT YOUR PARENTS TO BUY YOU AN E-READER?

Just remind them of a few fun facts. First, you have a portable library wherever you go. That beats hauling around every hardbound Harry Potter novel during your vacation. Second, many e-readers for kids feature a dictionary. So you are sure to rock your vocab tests. Third, you can use a keyboard to write on the electronic pages. That has to beat your pencil scribbles, right?

E-readers are portable. And they sure don't weigh as much as Gutenberg's Bible!

SMARTPHONES

Want to make a phone call and send some e-mail? Feel like taking a picture of your BFF? Maybe you would rather watch a movie or play a game. Just tap on the screen of your smartphone. You can do all these things and more with the same device!

A smartphone is a cell phone with a mobile operating system. It's like having a PC, camera, phone, GPS, music player, and more all in one. Frank J. Canova Jr. invented the first smartphone. It was called Simon.

By the 1990s, the world already knew about chips and going wireless. Canova wanted to squeeze some of that technology into a palm-sized package. He knew people would love a cell phone that let them do a million things on the go.

Canova was in the right place at the right time. He worked for IBM. The company liked Canova's ideas. So IBM started selling Simon in 1993. At first this new technology came with a pretty big price tag. Simon cost about $900!

Since then smartphones have become a lot cheaper. By 2012 more than one billion people were using smartphones. You may be thinking that smartphones can do everything except clean your room and walk the dog. (Maybe inventors will find a way to fix that next!) Sit tight if you don't have a smartphone yet. The odds are that you will someday. Experts say most cell phone companies will one day sell nothing but smartphones.

A smartphone is like an MP3 player, a television, a movie theater, a laptop, and a telephone all in one small package.

When your great-grandparents wanted to call their friends, they didn't whip out their smartphones. They used a big wall-mounted phone like this one.

TABLET COMPUTERS

Did you know that science fiction has led to some pretty cool hi-tech computers? Characters in many sci-fi movies, books, and TV shows in the 1960s had tablet computers. Of course, it would still take several years before tablets went from being make-believe technology to a real-life invention. The first real tablet was developed in Europe in 1994. In the United States, Intel made the Web Tablet in the 1990s.

It took a while for people to go gaga for tablets. Sure, they liked the idea of a touch-screen PC for folks on the go. But early tablets were too bulky.

So inventors crammed better technology into a tablet that would be smaller and easier to carry. Did their hard work pay off? Fans of the iPad think so. Apple released this tablet in 2010. It scored points for having a super-small touch screen plus a ton of applications.

The iPad and other tablets make it easy to surf the Web while you sit, stand, or run in a circle. Feel like watching a movie or listening to your favorite band? Just let your fingers fly across that nifty touch screen.

Plus, now you don't have to die of boredom while you wait in line with your parents at the grocery store. Tons of people ahead of you at the supermarket? Simply whip out your tablet and start browsing for an early birthday gift online. Or maybe catch up on that new book everyone in your class is talking about. The possibilities are endless and just a tap or two away on your tablet!

GLOSSARY

arcade: a building where people play coin-operated video games

calculate: to solve problems that deal with numbers, amounts, or time

console: a piece of equipment with a screen that people use to control a computer

digital: a system of electric signals that carry information

graphical user interface (GUI): a program with pictures, menus, a mouse, and a keyboard that are used to give directions to a computer

laser printer: a printer that uses laser beams to create words or pictures

motion sensor: a machine that detects movement

satellite: an object that people put into space to gather information and send signals back to Earth

scan: to move a beam of light over a surface to create an image of that surface

static electricity: electricity that occurs when two objects touch or rub against each other

virtual: sights and sounds that computers create to seem as realistic as possible

FURTHER INFORMATION

BrainPOP: Computer History
http://www.brainpop.com/technology/computers/computerhistory/preview.weml
Head to this page to check out an animated history of computers.

Doeden, Matt. *Steve Jobs: Technology Innovator and Apple Genius.*
Minneapolis: Lerner Publications Company, 2012. Find out more about the man who revolutionized the way we use computers.

The Federal Communications Commission (FCC): Kids Zone
http://transition.fcc.gov/cgb/kidszone/history.html
Check out this page to learn more about the background of inventions such as TV and the Internet.

Firestone, Mary. *Wireless Technology*. Minneapolis: Lerner Publications Company, 2009. Find out more about the wonders of wireless communication, from GPS to smartphones.

KidsHealth: Internet Safety
http://kidshealth.org/kid/watch/house/internet_safety.html
Review this site for a few easy-to-remember tips on Internet safety.

McPherson, Stephanie Sammartino. *Tim Berners-Lee: Inventor of the World Wide Web*. Minneapolis: Twenty-First Century Books, 2010. Read more about the man who changed the way people use the Internet.

Mitra, Ananda. *Digital Games: Computers at Play*. New York: Chelsea House, 2010. Read about the history and future of video games.

The Public Broadcasting Service (PBS): The Video Game Revolution
http://www.pbs.org/kcts/videogamerevolution/history
Visit this website for more information on how inventors developed video games.

Quinlan, Julia J. *GPS and Computer Maps*. New York: PowerKids Press, 2012. Learn more about how you can use GPS to get where you're going.

Science News for Kids
http://www.sciencenewsforkids.org/2008/09 /where-rivers-run-uphill-2
Check out this site for an interesting article on how scientists are using GPS to carry out research in Antarctica.

Technology for Kids
http://www.sciencekids.co.nz/technology.html
Visit this page for fast facts, videos, and word searches about inventions such as the Internet, video games, and cell phones.

Wyckoff, Edwin Brit. *The Man Who Invented Television: The Genius of Philo T. Farnsworth*. Berkeley Heights, NJ: Enslow Elementary, 2013. Read up on the young inventor who developed TV.

INDEX

PHOTO ACKNOWLEDGMENTS

The images in this book are used with the permission of: Illustrations by © Laura Westlund/Independent Picture Services; © Jamie Grill/Getty Images, p. 5 (bottom); © Adam Berry/Stringer/Getty Images, p. 5 (top); © Buddy Mays/Alamy, p. 7 (top); © Imagemore Co., Ltd/Getty Images, p. 7 (middle); © SSPL/The Image Works, p. 7 (bottom); © Bettmann/CORBIS, p. 9 (top); © iStockphoto.com/wdstock, pp. 9 (bottom), 17 (middle), 19 (top), 25 (middle); © ClassicStock/Alamy, p. 11 (top); © OJO Images/Getty Images, p. 11 (bottom); Courtesy of the Computer History Museum, pp. 13, 29 (top); © Joe McNally/Getty Images, p. 15 (right); Terry Schmitt/UPI/Newscom, p. 15 (left); © iStockphoto.com/nicholas belton, p. 15 (top); © Interfoto/Alamy, p. 17 (top); © Kidstock/Blend Images/Getty Images, p. 17 (bottom); © Hasloo Group Production Studio/Shutterstock.com, p. 19 (middle); © Andrew Brusso/CORBIS, p. 19 (bottom); © Charles Bowman/Stock Image/Getty Images, p. 21 (top); © Britain on View/Getty Images, p. 21 (middle); © Ed Bock/CORBIS, p. 21 (bottom); © Willie B. Thomas/Vetta/Getty Images, p. 23 (top); © Bettmann/CORBIS, p. 23 (bottom); The Beinecke Rare Book and Manuscript Library, Yale University, p. 25 (top); © VstockLLC/Getty Images, p. 25 (bottom); © Caroline Purser/Photographer's Choice/Getty Images, p. 27 (top); © Bettmann/CORBIS, p. 27 (bottom); © Age Fotostock/SuperStock, p. 29 (bottom).
Front cover: iStockphoto/Thinkstock.

Main body text set in Highlander ITC Std Book 13/16.
Typeface provided by International Typeface Corp.